FRESHWATER AQUARIUM FISH

FRESHWATER AQUARIUM FISH

CHARTWELL
BOOKS, INC.

Published by Chartwell Books
A Division of Book Sales Inc.
114 Northfield Avenue
Edison, New Jersey 08837
USA

0-7858-0968-6

This book is produced by
Quantum Books Ltd
6 Blundell Street
London N7 9BH

Project Manager: Rebecca Kingsley
Project Editor: Judith Millidge
Design/Editorial: David Manson
Andy McColm, Maggie Manson

The material in this publication previously appeared in
The Tropical Marine Fish Survival Guide,
An Illustrated Encyclopedia of Aquarium Fish,
The Aquarium Fish Survival Manual

QUMSPFF
Set in Futura
Reproduced in Singapore by United Graphic Ltd
Printed in Singapore by Star Standard Industries (Pte) Ltd

Contents

UNDERSTANDING
FRESHWATER FISH

Fish have managed to colonize
most bodies of water, from the
deepest oceans to the highest
mountain pool. All you have to
do is think about a place where
you find water and it is virtually
certain that you'll find a fish
that lives in it.

Anatomy of Freshwater Fish

Water is much denser than air, so fish's bodies are streamlined to pass through it. Most fish have torpedo-shaped bodies to enable smoother swimming, but fish from fast waters have flat bodies and expanded fins to improve their stability in the rushing currents.

BASIC ANATOMY

A fish's body is usually covered by scales or thick skin which afford protection. Their fins keep them upright, and provide foward power and steering. In order to maintain a certain position in the water, a fish uses its gas-filled, swim bladder which extends from behind the head for about a third of the body length. Combined with fatty tissues it gives the fish lift. The great majority of fish breathe by extracting the dissolved oxygen from water passing over their gills. In these organs the blood vessels are close to the surface allowing oxygen to be absorbed and waste gases to be exchanged.

Left: The all-round vision of midwater fish helps to provide an early warning of danger.

Above: Corydoras sterbai uses its barbels to sift the sandy substrate for food.

TASTE AND SMELL

Although fish have nostrils, they are not used for breathing but for smelling. Fish can smell food from distance; but to taste it they have to touch it. There is no single organ of taste. Instead taste receptors are scattered across the head and body surface. Barbels are also covered in taste receptors which allow the fish to feel through the silty substrate until it touches food.

VISION

Most fish have eyes, although they don't have eyelids. The position of the eyes is an indicator of lifestyle. Bottom dwellers have eyes on the top of their heads while midwater fish have eyes on the sides of their heads to provide all-round vision. Some predators have developed binocular vision but the eyes of some cave-inhabiting species have regressed so that they are now blind.

Aquatic Environments

When we think of freshwater fish, we envisage the minnows in our local stream or the trout and salmon on the fishmonger's slab. However, anywhere there is water you will find fish adapting to their environment.

UNDERGROUND FISH

Much of our fresh water is stored in natural underground aquifers, yet in these seemingly inhospitable conditions we find fish which inhabit caves and live their whole lives in darkness. Even where these undergound water sources emerge as sulphurous hot springs there are fish to be found.

RAINY SEASON FISH

Many pools and small rivers are seasonal—they dry out each year and are only refilled by monsoon rains. These waters are generally slow-moving and low in oxygen, becoming progressively harder during evaporation. Killifish inhabit such seasonal pools and bury their fertilized eggs to survive the temporary drought.

Left: Even in the most inhospitable regions fish can be found.

Above: The Mudskipper needs a special brackish water aquarium with a shore-like beach area.

FOREST CREEK FISH

For the aquarist it is a challenge to try to re-create some of the environments in the home aquarium. A forest creek, for example, with leaf litter on the substrate, plants which grow out of the water and dappled lighting would be home to some of the Banjo Catfish, which mimic leaf litter, or to the Splash Tetras which lay eggs on the undersides of broad leaves above the water.

BRACKISH WATER FISH

Consider the brackish water regions where we find Mudskippers. An aquarium set up for these fish would utilize wood in the form of roots coming down into the water and a sloping silty wave-washed area for the fish to slither out onto where they can display to each other. In contrast, you may wish to keep the Archer Fish that will spit at insects from his watery lair.

Choosing an Aquarium

Just wandering round your local aquatic retailer will give you an idea of the number of different aquaria that are available. The question is, which one will enhance your home and provide the right environment for your fish?

SELECTING A TANK

The first thing to consider is size. The larger the aquarium, the easier it is to manage. However, the maximum size will be determined by the site you have available in your house. If possible, position the aquarium away from a heat source such as a radiator or where direct sunlight will fall on it. Alcoves are a popular choice but, with larger modern homes, aquaria are sometimes used as room dividers. If a ready-made tank is not quite the right shape or size, a custom-built aquarium may be ordered, although the cost is usually higher.

Left: Tanks come in all shapes and sizes. Some are mounted on display stands and have hoods.

Above: Rockwork in an aquarium can be dramatic— but very heavy. Make sure your tank is strong enough.

ACID AND ALKALI LEVELS

The degree of acidity or alkalinity of water is referred to as pH. The pH range is from 0 (very acid) to 14 (very alkaline), with 7 the mid-point being referred to as neutral. The pH scale is logarithmic, therefore a change of one unit represents a 10-fold change. Most fish need a pH range of 6.5–8.5. The individual pH level for each fish is given in the Fish Species section (see p. 16).

WATER HARDNESS

The degree of water hardness is grad-ed by the amount of dissolved salts in the water and is referred to as °dH. The dH range is from 3° (very soft) to 25° (very hard). Most fish adapt to a range of 9–14°. However, some fish require very precise conditions, which must be provided, if you are to keep them successfully. Individual dH lev-els are given in the Fish Species sec-tion (see p. 16).

Decorating the Tank

What you use to decorate your aquarium is a purely personal choice. It will depend on the type of environment you wish to create. Dramatic effects can be achieved by using lots of different decorations, but be sure your tank is strong enough.

GRAVEL

Three sizes are available: fine grit, pea gravel and road surface gravel for larger aquaria.

ROCKS

Inert rocks such as slate, granite, and Westmoreland stone will not change the composition of your water.

Left: A well-planted tank needs only the addition of fish to bring it to life.

Above: *For the best effects choose plants that complement each other.*

WOOD

For versatility, wood is hard to beat in the aquarium. Not only is it decorative, it also provides an anchorage point for plants. For those who do not wish to use the real thing, realistic looking ceramic wood is available.

ARTIFICIAL PLANTS

Many of the artificial plants available today are so realistic that you can easily confuse them with the real thing. However, they are purely decorative and do not enhance the water quality of the aquarium or help combat any algal problems. Nevertheless,

they can look very attractive and provided your filtration system is well established there should be no problems.

LIVE PLANTS

In comparison, live plants can present more difficulties. First, you must carefully select truly aquatic species. Consider what you would do for garden plants. Plan your ideas on paper first and always leave sufficent space between individual plants for future growth. Make sure you plant them properly and give them sufficient light and good water conditions.

FISH SPECIES

Key to symbols

The following icons are used throughout this directory to help provide a snapshot of the idiosyncrasies of each species.

Size. Maximum adult length in inches.

Herbivore. Should only be fed vegetable-based foods

Omnivore. Eats all types of aquarium foods

Predator. A meat-eater likely to attack other fish.

Single specimen. Should not be kept with others of the same species.

Community. Can be kept in groups of its own kind.

Safe with smaller fish. Even if large species itself.

ANABAS TESTUDINEUS

These fish can travel across land, on their pectoral fins, when their habitats dry up. They have been found up trees, which is where their common name comes from—Climbing Perch.

Family Anabantidae.
Common name Climbing Perch.
Distribution Malaysia, Indonesia, India, Southern China.
Size 9in (22.5cm).
Food Omnivorous. Flake, live, or frozen aquatic invertebrates, vegetable matter.
Temperature 72–82°F (22–28°C).
pH 7.0–8.0 **dH** to 25°.

BETTA IMBELLIS

Best kept in groups that include males and females. The males can be kept together but will engage in mock fights and displays, although little damage will be done to either fish.

Family Belontidae.
Common name None.
Distribution Indonesia.
Size 2in (5cm).
Food Omnivorous. Live food preferred but will take flake and frozen food.
Temperature 75–77°F (24–25°C).
pH 7.0 **dH** to 10°.

BELONTIA HASSELTI

A peaceful fish unless spawning, when males become pugnacious, and lose the lace-like pattern on the fins. The female should be removed after spawning takes place.

Family Belontidae.
Common name None.
Distribution Singapore, Sumatra, Java, Borneo.
Size 7.5in (19cm).
Food Omnivorous. Predominantly meaty foods, plus vegetable matter.
Temperature 77–82°F (25–28°C).
pH 6.5–8.0 **dH** to 35°.

BELONTIA SIGNATA

A very hardy fish, can be aggressive, and should only be placed with fish which can defend themselves. Males have an extended dorsal fin.

Family Belontidae.
Common name Combtail.
Distribution Sri Lanka.
Size 5in (12.5cm).
Food Omnivorous. Live food preferred flake, vegetable matter.
Temperature 75–82°F (24–28°C).
pH 6.5–7.5 **dH** to 25°.

COLISA LABIOSA

A good fish for the community aquarium. Should be kept as pairs. Males are more colorful and have a pointed dorsal fin.

Family Belontidae.
Common name Thick-lipped Gourami.
Distribution Northern India, Burma.
Size 3.5in (9cm).
Food Omnivorous. Live, flaked and frozen food plus vegetable matter.
Temperature 72–82°F (22–28°C).
pH 6.0–7.5 **dH** to 10°.

COLISA FASCIATA

A beautiful fish, for the community aquarium, which should be bought and kept as pairs. Males have elongated bodies, are more colorful and their dorsal fin ends in a point.

Family Belontidae.
Common name Banded Gourami, Indian Gourami.
Distribution India to Burma.
Size 4in (10in).
Food Omnivorous. Live, flake, frozen food.
Temperature 72–82°F (22–28°C).
pH 6.0–7.5 **dH** to 15°.

MACROPODUS OCELLATUS

This fish is ideal for the home aquarium but is seldom imported. The male finnage is spectacular, both dorsal and anal fins are extended and the caudal is bright red-orange.

Family Belontidae.
Common name None.
Distribution Eastern China, Korea, Vietnam.
Size 3in (7.5cm).
Food Omnivorous. Live, flaked and frozen food.
Temperature 59–72°F (15–22°C).
pH 6.0–7.5 **dH** to 25°.

3

TRICHOGASTER LEERI

A wonderful fish for the larger community aquarium. Keep as pairs and they will display to each other, showing their true colors. Males show more red on the body.

Family Belontidae.
Common name Pearl, Gourami, Leeri.
Distribution Malaysia, Sumatra, Burma.
Size 4.5in (11cm).
Food Omnivorous. Flake, frozen, live and frozen food.
Temperature 75–82°F (24–28°C).
pH 6.5–8.0 **dH** to 30°.

4.5

PELTEOBAGRUS ORNATUS

P. ornatus is one of the few diurnally active Catfish. Its body is transparent to such a degree that not only are their internal organs visible, but so too are the body markings on the opposite side.

Family Bagridae.
Common name Dwarf Ornate Bagrid.
Distribution Malaysia and Indonesia.
Size 1.5in (4cm).
Food Insectivorous. Partial to *Daphnia* and *Tubifex*, will accept flake.
Temperature 72–77°F (22–25°C).
pH 6.5–7.2 **dH** 8–18°.

BROCHIS BRITSKII

This species has only been recently discovered, and is similarly colored to the other two species of *Brochis*. Unique among the Callichthyidae, *B. britskii* has a bony shield that completely covers the underside of the head.

Family Callichthyidae.
Common name None.
Distribution Brazil.
Size 3in (7.5cm).
Food Omnivorous.
Temperature 72–77°F (22–25°C).
pH 6.7–7.2 **dH** 8–20°.

ROCHIS MULTIRADIATUS

The very distinctive snout helps differentiate this species from other Brochis species. Sexing is not known and there is no spawning record. This species is fond of digging in search of its food.

Family Callichthyidae.
Common name Hog-nosed Brochis.
Distribution Ecuador.
Size 3.5in (9cm)
Food Omnivorous.
Temperature 72–75°F (22–24°C).
pH 6.5–7.2 **dH** 8–20°.

BROCHIS SPLENDENS

This fish is often confused with *Corydoras aeneus*, the Bronze Corydoras, which is similarly pigmented. However, the longer dorsal fin of *Brochis*, and its larger size, distinguish the two.

Family Callichthyidae.
Common name Sailfin Corydoras.
Distribution Brazil, Peru, Ecuador.
Size 3in (7.5cm).
Food Omnivorous. Like small aquatic invertebrates, flake food.
Temperature 70–80°F (21–27°C).
pH 6.0–7.5 **dH** 6–25°.

CORYDORAS PANDA

Juvenile specimens are more markedly colored than adults. *C. panda* is not so robust in captivity as other *Corydoras* species, requiring particular attention to water quality.

Family Callichthyidae.
Common name Panda Corydoras.
Distribution Peru.
Size 1.5in (4cm).
Food Omnivorous.
Temperature 72–79°F (22–26°C).
pH 6.5–7.5 **dH** 6–20°.

CORYDORAS BARBATUS

This is the largest species of the *Corydoras*. Those from the Rio de Janeiro area are more colorful, particularly the males which exhibit bright gold-yellow reticulations on the head.

Family Callichthyidae.
Common name Barbatus Catfish.
Distribution Brazil.
Size 2.5in (6cm).
Food Omnivorous.
Temperature 72–79°F (22–26°C).
pH 6.2–7.8 **dH** 4–25°.

DIANEMA LONGIBARBIS

Dianema are fairly peaceful, and not as boisterous as their *Hoplosternum* and *Callichthys* relatives. They are best kept in small groups of six or more, and tend to mope if isolated from others.

Family Callichthyidae.
Common name Porthole Catfish.
Distribution Peru.
Size 6in (15cm).
Food Omnivorous/Insectivorous.
Temperature 72–79°F (22–26°C).
pH 6.5–7.2 **dH** 7–20°.

DIANEMA UROSTRIATA

Clearly identifiable from *D. longibarbis* by the distinctive striped caudal fin. *D. urostriata* can also grow slightly larger than it. Both species are able to take in atmospheric air to supplement their oxygen supply.

Family Callichthyidae.
Common name Flag-tailed Catfish.
Distribution Brazil.
Size 6in (15cm).
Food Omnivorous/Insectivorous.
Temperature 72–79°F (22–26°C).
pH 6.2–7.2 **dH** 7–20°.

HOPLOSTERNUM LITTORALE

This is the largest member of the Callichthyidae family of Catfish. The slightly forked caudal fin helps distinguish this from other species of *Hoplosternum*.

Family Callichthyidae.
Common name None.
Distribution Northern South America.
Size 8in (20cm).
Food Omnivorous.
Temperature 70–80°F (21–27°C).
pH 6.2–7.5 **dH** 8–20°.

HOPLOSTERNUM THORACATUM

Found in muddy stretches of rivers and streams, *H. thoracatum's* auxiliary intestinal breathing allows it to survive in poorly oxygenated water. Coloration varies considerably with this fish, dependent on its locality.

Family Callichthyidae.
Common name None.
Distribution Northern South America.
Size 7in (17.5cm).
Food Omnivorous.
Temperature 70–80°F (21–27°C).
pH 6.5–7.5 **dH** 6–22°.

AGAMYXIS PECTINIFRONS

A sedentary catfish that fits in well in a community aquarium of medium to large peaceful fish. It spends much of its time hiding away in caves or crevices in wood. Most active at dusk and in the night.

Family Doradidae.
Common name Spotted Doras.
Distribution Ecuador.
Size 5.5in (14cm).
Food Omnivorous. Flake, tablet, frozen, live food.
Temperature 70–79°F (21–26°C).
pH 5.5–7.5 **dH** to 12°.

AMBLYDORAS HANCOCKI

A fairly placid fish, *A. hancocki* can be kept in a community tank of similar sized fish. The common name alludes to the noises it produces when communicating.

Family Doradidae.
Common name Talking Catfish.
Distribution Northern South America.
Size 4.5in (11cm).
Food Omnivorous. Flake, commercial fish food.
Temperature 72–80°F (22–27°C).
pH 6.5–7.5 **dH** 8–16°.

MEGALODORUS IRWINI

Growth in the aquarium can be slow, but the fish is long-lived. As it grows, so too do the lateral plates and the thorn on each. The dorsal and pectoral fins are equipped with serrations.

Family Doradidae.
Common name Snail-eating Doradid.
Distribution Brazilian Amazon.
Size 24in (60cm).
Food Carnivorous. Snails, pelleted food, chopped earthworms, beef-heart.
Temperature 72–79°F (22–26°C).
pH 6.5–7.4 **dH** 7–20°.

HYPANCISTRUS ZEBRA

When photographs were first published of this fish, there was a rush by Catfish enthusiasts to obtain specimens. They have now become more readily available.

Family Loricariidae.
Common name Zebra Plec, L46.
Distributio Brazil.
Size 3in (7.5cm).
Food Omnivorous. Prefers meaty foods.
Temperature 72–80°F (22–27°C).
pH 6.4–7.0 **dH** 5–12°.

PANAQUE NIGROLINEATUS

Adult males can fight, using their
interopercular spines as weapons.
There are a number of variations of
patterning which may be regional
differences of the same species or
new species in their own right.

Family Loricariidae.
Common name Pin-striped Plec.
Distribution Colombia.
Size 10in (25cm).
Food Herbivorous.
Temperature 72–79°F (22–26°C).
pH 6.5–7.5 **dH** 5–18°.

PIMELODUS PICTUS

The sharp pectoral and dorsal spines
make it difficult to handle this fish.
A net should never be used to catch
these fish as the spines will become
entangled and removal is difficult.
Plastic bags are preferable.

Family Pimelodidae.
Common name Angelicus Pim.
Distribution Colombia.
Size 4.5in (11cm).
Food Insectivorous. Flake, tablet food.
Temperature 72–77°F (22–25°C).
pH 6.0–6.8 **dH** to 12°.

APHYOCHARAX ANISITSI

An undemanding shoal fish that may be kept in an unheated aquarium. However, if kept at the cooler end of its range the colors fade. A long-lived species and a good fish for the beginner.

Family Characidae.
Common name Bloodfin.
Distribution Argentina.
Size 2in(5cm).
Food Omnivorous. Small live or frozen food, flake.
Temperature 64–81°F (18–28°C).
pH 6.0–8.0 **dH** to 28°.

ASTYANAX FASCIATUS MEXICANUS

This fish is widely available in the hobby, far more so than its sighted counterpart. It is undemanding, should be kept in shoals and makes an excellent community fish.

Family Characidae.
Common name Blind Cavefish.
Distribution Texas, Mexico, Panama.
Size 3.5in (9cm).
Food Omnivorous. Flake, live or frozen food.
Temperature 72–77°F (22–25°C).
pH 6.0–8.0 **dH** to 30°.

CHALCEUS MACROLEPIDOTUS

A large predatory Characin for the specialist. Easy to keep in a large tank, but fit a tight cover because the fish are prone to jumping. Can be kept with fish of a similar size.

Family Characidae.
Common name Pink-tailed Chalceus.
Distribution Northern South America.
Size 10in (25cm).
Food Carnivorous. Takes meat, fish and tablet food.
Temperature 73–81°F (23–27°C).
pH 6.5–7.5 **dH** to 18°.

CORYNOPOMA RIISEI

A gentle shoaling fish for the community aquarium. Can be difficult to acclimatize, but once used to aquarium conditions it is very robust. Males have longer pectoral fins.

Family Characidae.
Common name Swordtail Characin.
Distribution Colombia.
Size 2.5in (6cm).
Food Omnivorous. Live, flake and frozen food.
Temperature 72–81°F (22–27°C).
pH 6.0–7.5 **dH** to 25°.

GYMNOCORYMBUS SOCOLOFI

Juveniles, up to 1.5in (4cm) long, are very attractive and active; their unpaired fins are red-orange in color. However, this fades with maturity and the fish become more sedate.

Family Characidae.
Common name Socolof's Tetra.
Distribution Colombia.
Size 2in (5cm).
Food Omnivorous. Flake, insect larvae, vegetable matter.
Temperature 72–79°F (22–26°C).
pH 5.5–7.5 **dH** to 20°.

HEMMIGRAMMUS ERYTHROZONUS

Peaceful, shoaling fish for the planted community aquarium. Males are slimmer than females. This fish is bred commercially in large numbers. It is friendly with its own species and safe with smaller fish.

Family Characidae.
Common name Glowlight Tetra.
Distribution Guyana.
Size 1.5in (4cm).
Food Omnivorous. Flake, insect larvae.
Temperature 72–79°F (22–26°C).
pH 6.0–7.5 **dH** to 15°.

HEMIGRAMMUS ULREYI

A timid fish when first introduced into the aquarium. Needs plenty of space and the company of other peaceful species. They display their best colors when seen in sunlight.

Family Characidae.
Common name Ulrey's Tetra.
Distribution Paraguay.
Size 2in (5cm).
Food Omnivorous. Flake, insect larvae, and small aquatic invertebrates.
Temperature 73–81°F (23–27°C).
pH 6.0–7.0 **dH** to 10°.

HYPHESSOBRYCON PULCHRIPINNIS

A pretty shoaling fish for the community aquarium, always swimming about. It is friendly with its own species and safe with smaller fish as well. Males have a black edge to the anal fin.

Family Characidae.
Common name Lemon Tetra.
Distribution Peru.
Size 2in (5cm).
Food Omnivorous. Live, frozen, flake.
Temperature 73–81°F (23–27°C).
pH 6.0–7.5 **dH** to 20°.

MOENKHAUSIA PITTERI

A shoaling fish for the well-planted community aquarium. Feed well on live foods such as *Daphnia*, blood-worm, and mosquito larvae, or frozen substitutes.

Family Characidae.
Common name Diamond Tetra.
Distribution Venezuela.
Size 2.5in (6cm).
Food Omnivorous. Flake, live *Daphnia*, small frozen invertebrates.
Temperature 75–82°F (24–28°C).
pH 5.5–7.0 **dH** 4–10°.

PARACHEIRODON INNESI

Probably the most popular of all aquarium fish, Neons are bred in vast numbers and tolerate a wide range of aquarium conditions. Males are slim and have a straight blue line.

Family Characidae.
Common name Neon Tetra.
Distribution Peru.
Size 1.5in (4cm).
Food Omnivorous. Flake, insect larvae, small frozen invertebrates.
Temperature 68–79°F (20–26°C).
pH 7.0 **dH** to 20°.

CHARACINS

HARACIDIUM RACHOVII

eaceful with other fish. Loach-like in
's habits and movements. Males have
a spotted dorsal fin; females have a
ransparent dorsal fin.

amily Characidae.
Common name None.
Distribution Southern Brazil.
Size 3in (7.5cm).
Food Carnivorous. Tablet food, live
or frozen insect larvae.
Temperature 68–75°F (20–24°C).
pH 5.5–7.5 **dH** to 24°.

CURIMATA SPILURA

Very peaceful fish for the larger community aquarium, provided that the
plants are hardy enough to withstand
the onslaught. Copious amounts of
green foods should be offered.

Family Curimatidae.
Common name Diamond-spot
Curimata.
Distribution South America.
Size 3.5in (9cm).
Food Herbivorous. Vegetable foods,
but will take flake.
Temperature 70–81°F (21–27°C).
pH 6.0–7.5 **dH** to 25°.

AEQUIDENS RIVULATUS

Noted for its aggression, they should be kept only with fish able to fend for themselves. They take up territories and will defend them especially when breeding. Males are generally larger, females are darker in color.

Family Cichlidae.
Common name Green Terror.
Distribution Ecuador, Peru.
Size 8in (20cm).
Food Omnivorous. Live food if possible, will take flake or frozen food.
Temperature 70–75°F (21–24°C).
pH 6.5–7.5 **dH** to 15°.

AMPHILOPHUS ALFARI

Variations can be seen in the color, body, and finnage shape of this fish, even in fish from the same river system. In the aquarium it is domineering and also likes to dig in the substrate. Males are much larger than females.

Family Cichlidae.
Common name Pastel Cichlid.
Distribution Central America.
Size 9in (22.5cm).
Food Omnivorous. Live, flake, frozen food.
Temperature 73–79°F (23–26°C).
pH 6.5–7.0 **dH** to 10°.

AMPHILOPHUS CITRINELLUS

This is a rather belligerent fish especially when breeding. They love to dig and move large quantities of gravel around the aquarium, so plants in the aquarium are a waste of space.

Family Cichlidae.
Common name Midas Cichlid.
Distribution Central America.
Size 12in (30cm).
Food Omnivorous. Live, flake, frozen.
Temperature 73–79°F (23–26°C).
pH 6.5–7.0 **dH** to 10°.

APISTOGRAMMA BORELLII

A beautiful fish that makes a lovely addition to a well-balanced, community aquarium of very peaceful fish. These creatures are territorial but problems only arise when they are breeding.

Family Cichlidae.
Common name Borelli's Dwarf Cichlid.
Distribution S. America.
Size 3in (7.5cm).
Food Carnivorous. Small live food.
Temperature 75–77°F (24–25°C).
pH 6.0–6.5 **dH** to 12°.

APISTOGRAMMA CACATUOIDES

This fish derives its names from the extended rays at the beginning of the dorsal fin. Males are much larger than females and have longer fins. Keep several females with each male.

Family Cichlidae.
Common name Cockatoo Dwarf Cichlid.
Distribution Brazil.
Size 3.5in (9cm).
Food Carnivorous. Live food, flake.
Temperature 75–77°F (24–25°C).
pH 7.0 **dH** to 10°.

APISTOGRAMMA MACMASTERI

A delightful fish that has a wonderful territorial defensive display which can be seen quite often if the group is kept with a few other peaceful fish. Males are larger, the caudal is bright red.

Family Cichlidae.
Common name Macmaster's Dwarf Cichlid.
Distribution Venezuela.
Size 3in (7.5cm).
Food Carnivorous. Live food.
Temperature 75–86°F (24–30°C).
pH 6.0–6.5 **dH** to 8°.

APISTOGRAMMA NIJSSENI

A very beautiful fish that only shows its true potential if the correct water conditions can be maintained. Males are larger and colorful. Peaceful and may be kept with other fish.

Family Cichlidae.
Common name Nijssen's Dwarf Cichlid, Panda Dwarf Cichlid.
Distribution Peru.
Size 2.5in (6cm).
Food Carnivorous. Live food, flake, frozen.
Temperature 75–86°F (24–30°C).
pH 5.5 **dH** below 5°.

APISTOGRAMMA STEINDACHNERI

Only aggressive when spawning, these fish may be housed with other fish, but be prepared for the other fish to be herded to one section of the aquarium if the Cichlids breed. Males are larger and more colorful.

Family Cichlidae.
Common name Steindachner's Dwarf Cichlid.
Distribution Guyana.
Size 4in (10cm).
Food Carnivorous. Live food.
Temperature 73–77°F (23–25°C).
pH 6.0–7.0 **dH** to 10°.

C I C H L I D S

ARCHOCENTRUS NIGROFASCIATUS

An undemanding fish, but it is belligerent towards other fish and is therefore
most suited to a species aquarium. They
pair off and spawn readily. There is an
albino variety of this fish.

Family Cichlidae.
Common name Convict Cichlid,
Zebra Cichlid.
Distribution Central America.
Size 6in (15cm).
Food Omnivorous. Live, flake, frozen,
green food.
Temperature 68–75°F (20–24°C).
pH 6.5–8.0 **dH** to 20°.

ARCHOCENTRUS SPILURUS

Very peaceful, they will breed regularly
if conditions are right. Males are larger
with a pointed dorsal and ventral fins.
Mature males have a bump on their
foreheads.

Family Cichlidae.
Common name None.
Distribution Guatemala.
Size 4.5in (11cm).
Food Omnivorous. Live, flake, frozen,
green food.
Temperature 72–77°F (22–25°C).
pH 6.5–7.5 **dH** to 12°.

ASTATOTILAPIA BURTONI

A territorial and quarrelsome fish with its own kind that lives quietly with other species. Keep several females with each male.

Family Cichlidae.
Common name Burton's Mouthbreeder.
Distribution East and Central Africa.
Size 4.5in (11cm).
Food Omnivorous. Live, flake, frozen, green food.
Temperature 68–75°F (20–24°C).
pH 8.0–9.0 **dH** to 20°.

AULONOCARA BAENSCHI

The males of this striking fish are yellow and blue, the degree of one or other of the colors depends on the locality the fish are from. Peaceable and suitable for most community aquaria.

Family Cichlidae.
Common name Baensch's Peacock, Yellow Regal Cichild.
Distribution Malawi.
Size 4in (10cm).
Food Omnivorous. Live, flake, frozen food.
Temperature 72–77°F (22–25°C).
pH 7.5–8.5 **dH** to 25°.

C I C H L I D S

CICHLASOMA PORTALEGRENSIS

A hardy fish well suited to beginners, they are easy to keep, feed, and breed. It is not easy to tell the sexes unless the fish are ready to breed, males tend to be greenish in color while the female is brownish.

Family Cichlidae.
Common name Brown Acara, Port Acara.
Distribution Brazil, Bolivia, Paraguay.
Size 6in (15cm).
Food Omnivorous. Live, flake, frozen.
Temperature 66–75°F (19–24°C).
pH 6.0–7.0 **dH** to 10°.

CLEITHRACARA MARONII

Commercially bred, they are now becoming so inbred that their size has diminished. A peaceful fish, it is ideal for a larger community aquarium.

Family Cichlidae.
Common name Keyhole Cichlid.
Distribution Guyana.
Size 6in (15cm).
Food Omnivorous. Live, flake, frozen food.
Temperature 72–77°F (22–25°C).
pH 6.0–8.0 **dH** to 20°.

COPORA NICARAGUENSIS

In the main peaceful, *C. nicaraguensis* is a very beautiful fish that can be kept with other species. Their one drawback is that they eat some plants.

Family Cichlidae.
Common name Nicaragua Cichild.
Distribution Nicaragua, Cost Rica.
Size 10in (25cm).
Food Omnivorous. Live, flake, frozen food.
Temperature 73–79°F (23–26°C).
pH 7.0–8.0 **dH** to 15°.

YPRICHROMIS LEPTOSOMA

A shoaling fish, it requires a lot of swimming space in the upper levels of the aquarium. It may be kept with other cichilds as it is quite peaceful. Males are brownish with yellow tips to the pectoral fins.

Family Cichlidae.
Common name None.
Distribution Tanzania.
Size 5.5in (14cm).
Food Omnivorous. Live, flake, frozen food.
Temperature 73–77°F (23–25°C).
pH 8.0–9.0 **dH** to 20°.

GEOPHAGUS BRASILIENSIS

Although territorial, it is fairly tolerant of other fish. These fish are best left to pair themselves since, if the pair is incompatible, they may keep eating the eggs.

Family Cichlidae.
Common name Pearl Cichild.
Distribution Eastern Brazil.
Size 11in (27.5cm).
Food Omnivorous. Live, flake, frozen food.
Temperature 68–73°F (20–23°C).
pH 6.5–7.0 **dH** to 10°.

HEROTILAPIA MULTISPINOSA

These fish are like chameleons, they change color according to their mood. It is difficult to tell the sexes even though the male's fins tend to be pointed and longer.

Family Cichlidae.
Common name None.
Distribution Panama, Nicaragua.
Size 5in (12.5cm).
Food Omnivorous. Live, flake, frozen, green food.
Temperature 72–77°F (22–25°C).
pH 7.0 **dH** to 10°.

PSEUDOTROPHEUS SOCOLOFI

This peaceful creature is only defensive when breeding. The easiest way to tell the sexes is by the egg spots on the anal fin of the male.

Family Cichlidae.
Common name Eduard's Mbuna.
Distribution Malawi.
Size 4.5in (11cm).
Food Omnivorous. Live, flake, frozen food.
Temperature 75–79°F (24–26°C).
pH 8.0–8.5 **dH** to 18°.

SATANOPERCA ACUTICEPS

A beautiful, non-aggressive Cichild whose only drawback is that it likes to dig, it my be kept with other peaceful fish. Males have extended dorsal and anal fins.

Family Cichlidae.
Common name Sparkling Geophagus.
Distribution Brazil.
Size 10in (25cm).
Food Omnivorous. Live, flake, frozen, green food.
Temperature 75–79°F (24–26°C).
pH 6.5–7.0 **dH** to 12°.

HOMALOPTERA ORTHOGONIATA

Very peaceful with other fish; with each other there may be mock fights but no damage is done. They spend much time grazing through algae and over flat rocks and leaves.

Family Balitoridae.
Common name Saddled Hillstream Loach.
Distribution Indonesia, Thailand.
Size 4.5in (11cm).
Food Omnivorous. Aufwuchs, bloodworms.
Temperature 68–75°F (20–24°C).
pH 7.0 **dH** to 10°.

BOTIA BERDMOREI

A boisterous fish, it can be aggressive to its own kind and others, preventing them from feeding. When irate it may make clicking noises. Take care when handling.

Family Cobitidae.
Common name None.
Distribution Burma, Thailand.
Size 6in (15cm).
Food Omnivorous. Flake, frozen, live food.
Temperature 72–79°F (22–26°C).
pH 6.5–7.5 **dH** to 15°.

BOTIA MACRACANTHUS

A social Loach that should be kept in groups. It is active by day, and a worthy occupant for any community aquarium. The species is prone to White Spot.

Family Cobitidae.
Common name Clown Loach.
Distribution India, Sumatra, Borneo.
Size 6in (15cm).
Food Omnivorous. Flake, frozen, tablet, live foods.
Temperature 77–86°F (25–30°C).
pH 6.0–6.5 **dH** to 12°.

BARBUS BIMACULATUS

Classic shoaling fish that likes the company of its own kind. Kept in groups they will swim out in the open, but kept as solitary specimens or pairs they tend to retire to the darker recesses.

Family Cyprinidae.
Common name Two-Spot Barb.
Distribution Sri Lanka.
Size 3in (7.5cm).
Food Omnivorous. Flake, frozen, live food.
Temperature 72–75°F (22–24°C).
pH 6.5–7.0 **dH** to 15°.

C Y P R I N I D S

BARBUS LINEATUS

A very active shoaling fish that should be kept in groups of 10 or more. The lines on the male's body are more pronounced and he is slimmer than the female.

Family Cyprinidae.
Common name Striped Barb.
Distribution Malayasia.
Size 4.5in (11cm).
Food Omnivorous. Flake, frozen, live and green food.
Temperature 70–75°F (21–24°C).
pH 6.0–6.5 **dH** to 10°.

BARBUS SCHWANEFELDI

Although sold in great numbers for community aquaria, they are not really suited to this. They grow large and are very active. They are ideal when kept as a shoal in very large display tanks.

Family Cyprinidae.
Common name Tinfoil Barb, Schwanefeld's Barb.
Distribution S.E. Asia.
Size 14in (35cm).
Food Omnivorous. Flake, frozen, live and green food.
Temperature 72–77°F (22–25°C).
pH 6.5–7.0 **dH** to 10°.

BARBUS RHOMBOOCELLATUS

Seldom imported, this fish seems to do
well in soft, slightly acidic water. When
healthy and fed lots of live foods, these
fish have an almost iridescent sheen on
their body.

Family Cyprinidae.
Common name None.
Distribution Borneo.
Size 2in (5cm).
Food Omnivorous. Live foods or flake.
Temperature 73–82°F (23–28°C).
pH 6.5–7.5 **dH** to 10°.

BARBUS TICTO

Ideally suited to a community aquarium,
these fish are undemanding. They can
take cooler conditions in the winter but
before doing this check that your other
fish can tolerate such low conditions.

Family Cyprinidae.
Common name Ticto Barb, Two-Spot
Barb.
Distribution India, Sri Lanka.
Size 4in (10cm).
Food Omnivorous. Flake, frozen, live
foods.
Temperature 66–72°F (19–22°C).
pH 6.5 **dH** to 10°.

BRACHYDANIO NIGROFASCIATUS

These seem to prefer warmer waters than other *Brachydanio* species. Keep them as a shoal. Males are slimmer and their anal fin has a dark brown edge, which can appear golden.

Family Cyprinidae.
Common name Spotted Danio.
Distribution Burma.
Size 2in (5cm).
Food Omnivorous. Flake, frozen, live food.
Temperature 75–82°F (24–28°C).
pH 6.5–7.0 **dH** to 12°.

CYCLOCHEILICHTHYS JANTHOCHIR

An active fish, it likes plenty of space to swim in. Generally peaceful toward fish of a similar size. It makes an excellent companion for peaceful, bottom dwelling Catfish.

Family Cyprinidae.
Common name None.
Distribution Indonesia, Borneo.
Size 8in (20cm).
Food Omnivorous. Flake, frozen, live food.
Temperature 72–79°F (22–26°C).
pH 6.0–6.5 **dH** to 8°.

DANIO AEQUIPINNATUS

An excellent fish for the larger community aquarium. Keep in shoals of males and females. Males are slimmer, more intensely colored and have a blue stripe.

Family Cyprinidae.
Common name Giant Danio.
Distribution India, Sri Lanka.
Size 4in (10cm).
Food Omnivorous. Flake, frozen, live and vegetable food.
Temperature 72–75°F (22–24°C).
pH 6.0–7.0 **dH** to 12°.

NOTROPIS LUTRENSIS

A cold water fish, it is becoming more and more popular for the aquarium. Keep as a shoal. In the wild they live in moderately flowing streams which have a gravel or sand substrate.

Family Cyprinidae.
Common name Shiner.
Distribution Midwest USA.
Size 3.5in (9cm).
Food Omnivorous. Flake, frozen, live food.
Temperature 59–75°F (15–24°C).
pH 7.0–7.5 **dH** to 18°.

OPSARISIUM CHRYSTYI

A very attractive fish but seldom imported, it should be kept in groups. A surface dweller, it will jump at the least provocation. The colors in sunlight are unbelievable.

Family Cyprinidae.
Common name None.
Distribution Northern Ghana.
Size 6in (15cm).
Food Carnivorous. Aquatic invertebrates, insects or flake.
Temperature 72–75°F (22–24°C).
pH 6.5 **dH** to 10°.

PARLUCIOSOMA CEPHALOTAENIA

Classic shoaling fish that is often overlooked for the large community aquarium. It should be kept in groups of six or more individuals. Males are slimmer than females.

Family Cyprinidae.
Common name Porthole Rasbora.
Distribution S.E.Asia.
Size 5.5in (14cm).
Food Omnivorous. Flake, frozen, live food.
Temperature 72–75°F (22–24°C).
pH 6.0–6.5 **dH** to 15°.

RASBORA EINTHOVENII

A shoaling fish for the community aquarium. It is only possible to tell males and females apart during the breeding season. At this time males are smaller and slimmer.

Family Cyprinidae.
Common name Long-Band Rasbora.
Distribution S.E.Asia.
Size 3in (7.5cm).
Food Omnivorous. Live, flake and frozen food.
Temperature 72–77°F (22–25°C).
pH 6.0–6.5 **dH** to 8°.

RASBORA RETICULATA

A very attractive fish for the large community aquarium with open water and compatible with other peaceable fish of a similar size. Good glass cover is needed as they may jump.

Family Cyprinidae.
Common name Net Rasbora.
Distribution Sumatra.
Size 2.5in (6cm).
Food Omnivorous. Flake, frozen, live food.
Temperature 72–79°F (22–26°C).
pH 6.0–6.5 **dH** to 10°.

APHYOSEMION AUSTRALE

One of the most frequently seen killies, and an excellent fish for the softwater community aquarium. Males are far more colorful than females, and have extended finnage.

Family Aplocheilidae.
Common name Cape Lopez Lyretail.
Distribution West Africa.
Size 2.5in (6cm).
Food Omnivorous. Prefer live food but will take flake.
Temperature 70–75°F (21–24°C).
pH 5.5–6.5 **dH** to 10°.

APHYOSEMION CALLIURUM

Males can be quarrelsome with other males of their own kind. Females are plain in comparison with the highly colored males.

Family Aplocheilidae.
Common name Red-Seam Killie.
Distribution West Africa.
Size 2in (5cm).
Food Carnivorous. Will take flake and frozen food.
Temperature 75–79°F (24–26°C).
pH 6.5–7.0 **dH** to 15°.

KILLIFISH

APHYOSEMION SCHMITTI

These are peaceful fish that may be
kept with others of a similar nature.
Males are exceedingly colorful,
whereas females are brown with faint
red spots.

Family Aplocheilidae.
Common name Schmitt's Killie.
Distribution Liberia.
Size 2.5in (6cm).
Food Carnivorous. All small live food.
Temperature 72–75°F (22–24°C).
pH 6.0–6.5 **dH** to 8°.

APHYOSEMION GERYI

Easy to keep, this attractive fish may be
placed in a community aquarium.
Males are more colorful than females.
However, different populations have
differing degrees of coloration.

Family Aplocheilidae.
Common name None.
Distribution West Africa.
Size 2in (5cm).
Food Carnivorous. Prefer live food but
will take flake and frozen.
Temperature 72–79°F (22–26°C).
pH 5.5–6.5 **dH** to 10°.

BRACHYRHAPHIS EPISCOPI

A beautiful little livebearer, but very difficult to maintain for any length of time in captivity. It is susceptible to disease, so aquarium hygiene is all important.

Family Poecilidae.
Common name Bishop Brachy.
Distribution Central America.
Size 1.5in (4cm).
Food Carnivorous. All small live food, sometimes frozen food.
Temperature 75–79°F (24–26°C).
pH 7.0–8.0 **dH** 4–20°.

GAMBUSIA AFFINIS

Gregarious and undemanding, it may may be kept with other similar fish. Its almost insatiable appetite for mosquito larvae has lead this fish to be widely used for malaria control.

Family Poecilidae.
Common name Western Mosquitofish.
Distribution Texas.
Size 1.5in (4cm).
Food Carnivorous. Prefer live mosquito larvae but will take flake and frozen.
Temperature 64–75°F (18–24°C).
pH 6.0–8.0 **dH** to 30°.

GIRARDINUS FALCATUS

Very tolerant of most water conditions, this fish may be kept with other peaceful fish. Its name refers to the sickle-shaped gonopodium of the males.

Family Poecilidae.
Common name Yellow Belly.
Distribution Western Cuba.
Size 2in (5cm).
Food Omnivorous. Flake, frozen, live and green food.
Temperature 75–84°F (24–29°C).
pH 6.0–8.0 **dH** to 25°.

LIMIA VITTATA

An excellent fish for the hard water community aquarium. Males are more colorful, with black and gold spangles. Females have less intense coloration.

Family Poecilidae.
Common name Cuban Limia.
Distribution Cuba.
Size 4.5in (11cm).
Food Omnivorous. Algae, aquatic invertebrates, flake.
Temperature 72–79°F (22–26°C).
pH 7.5–8.5 **dH** 8–30°.

POECILIA LATIPINNA

A species which has been cultivated to produce various color forms. Suitable for a hard-water community aquarium, but best kept in brackish or marine water.

Family Poecilidae.
Common name Sailfin Molly.
Distribution Southern USA.
Size 4in (10cm).
Food Omnivorous. Algae, plant material plus live food and flake.
Temperature 68–82°F (20–28°C).
pH 7.5–8.5 **dH** 10–30°.

POECILIA RETICULATA

A highly adaptable fish that is a firm favorite among novices. Bred by the millions in fish farms, Guppies have been hybridized to give larger finnage on males.

Family Poecilidae.
Common name Guppy, Millionsfish.
Distribution Central America, Brazil.
Size 2.5in (6cm).
Food Omnivorous. Small aquatic invertebrates, flake.
Temperature 64–81°F (18–27°C).
pH 7.0–8.5 **dH** 4–30°.

XIPHOPHORUS MACULATUS

The ideal community fish, peaceful and fecund. Its young will even grow to maturity in a community tank. Many variant color forms have been produced.

Family Poecilidae.
Common name Southern Platy.
Distribution E. coast of Mexico, Guatemala, Honduras.
Size 4in (10cm).
Food Omnivorous. Small aquatic invertebrates, flake.
Temperature 72–79°F (22–26°C).
pH 7.0–8.0 **dH** 8–35°.

XIPHOPHORUS VARIATUS

A classic community fish. It can even be kept at low temperatures in an unheated aquarium, provided it is acclimatized to these conditions slowly.

Family Poecilidae.
Common name Variable Platy.
Distribution Southern Mexico.
Size 2in (5cm).
Food Omnivorous. Small aquatic invertebrates, flake.
Temperature 59–77°F (15–25°C).
pH 7.0–8.0 **dH** 8–35°.

CHILATHERINA AXELRODI

An active fish which displays well when kept as a shoal of males and females. Males are more colorful than females. Keep in a community aquarium with plenty of open water.

Family Melanotaeniidae.
Common name Axelrod's Rainbow.
Distribution Papua New Guinea.
Size 3.5in (9cm).
Food Omnivorous. Takes flake, frozen and live food.
Temperature 77–82°F (25–28°C).
pH 7.0–8.0 **dH** 12°.

CHILATHERINA FASCIATA

A rather attractive Rainbow, it likes brightly lit conditions, being found in areas of streams where sunlight falls. Males are larger and more colorful than females.

Family Melanotaeniidae.
Common name Barred Rainbow.
Distribution Northern New Guinea.
Size 4.5in(11cm).
Food Omnivorous. Prefers live food.
Temperature 81–86°F (27–30°C).
pH 7.0–8.0 **dH** to 10°.

GLOSSOLEPIS MACULOSUS

One of the smaller Rainbowfish, they may be combined with other peaceful fish. Keep them in shoals and pay careful attention to water quality. The spots appear at two to three months old.

Family Melanotaeniidae.
Common name Spotted Rainbow.
Distribution Papua New Guinea.
Size 2in (5cm).
Food Omnivorous. Takes flake, frozen and algae.
Temperature 75–79°F (24–26°C).
pH 7.5 **dH** to 12°.

MELANOTAENIA HERBERTAXELRODI

A peaceful shoaling fish. Males are deeper in the body and more colorful than females. The best colors are shown in sunlight.

Family Melanotaeniidae.
Common name Lake Tebera Rainbow.
Distribution Papua New Guinea.
Size 3.5in (9cm).
Food Omnivorous. Takes flake, frozen and live food.
Temperature 70–77°F (21–25°C).
pH 7.5–8.0 **dH** 10–15°.

MELANOTAENIA LACUSTRIS

Very eyecatching, these fish make a
wonderful focal point in an aquarium.
Males have the more intense blue
coloration. Unfortunately this color
fades slightly with successive captive-
bred generations.

Family Melanotaeniidae.
Common name Lake Kutubu Rainbow.
Distribution Papua New Guinea.
Size 4in (10cm).
Food Omnivorous. Takes flake, frozen
and live food.
Temperature 75–79°F (24–26°C).
pH 7.0–7.5 **dH** about 12°.

MELANOTAENIA PARKINSONI

Keep these active fish in a shoal.
These are one of the easier Rainbows
to keep, and they breed readily in the
community aquarium.

Family Melanotaeniidae.
Common name Parkinson's Rainbow.
Distribution Papua New Guinea.
Size 4.5in (11cm).
Food Omnivorous. Prefers live food but
takes flake and frozen.
Temperature 79–84°F (26–29°C).
pH 7.5–8.0 **dH** 8–15°.

Index

INDEX

Index of common names

DATE DUE

LGER McKINSEY ELEMENTARY SCHOOL
SEVERNA PARK, MD. 21146